INTRODUCTION

HMS *Alliance* was laid down at the Vickers Shipyard in Barrow-in-Furness on 13 March 1945. Allied forces had entered Germany and the defeat of Hitler's Third Reich was just weeks away. In the Far East, the war with Japan was at its height. HMS *Alliance* and the other A Class submarines under construction had been designed for the Pacific in World War Two. Following the dropping of atomic bombs on Hiroshima and Nagasaki by the United States in August 1945, the Japanese surrendered and the war was finally at an end. When HMS *Alliance* entered service in 1947, Britain was still subject to economic austerity and wartime rationing. The first signs of tension between the Western Allies and the Soviet Union were apparent and the British Empire was beginning to break up.

Over the next three decades, *Alliance* performed many different roles in the post-war Cold War era. She operated all over the world and many hundreds of submariners served in her during the course of her 26 years in commission. In 1958, her familiar appearance as a World War Two-era submarine changed dramatically when she was comprehensively modernised to meet the demands of Cold War submarine operations. *Alliance* was streamlined and made quieter and faster underwater because her new role included countering the submarines of the Soviet Union.

In 1973 *Alliance* was finally paid off at HMS *Dolphin* in Gosport, then the home of the Royal Navy Submarine Service. For a few years *Alliance* served as a static training submarine, but in 1979 the Navy embarked on the ambitious task of preserving *Alliance* as the last surviving submarine from World War Two. In 1982, HMS *Alliance* went on display to the public for the first time as an historic ship, and also as a memorial to more than 5,300 submariners who had given their lives serving in Royal Navy submarines.

WORLD WAR TWO

In 1939, at the outbreak of World War Two, the Royal Navy did not possess any submarines specially suited for operation in the Far East. The climate and sheer size of the Pacific Ocean meant that submarines operating in that theatre needed greater endurance and improved crew habitability. In the Pacific, a submarine might take up to a week just to reach her patrol area, while the heat and humidity was a constant challenge to the efficiency and health of the crew. The A Class were specifically designed for Far East operations and there were a number of key features incorporated into the design. *Alliance* was bigger and faster than previous Royal Navy designs, and most of the crew accommodation was located forward of the noise and smell of the Engine Room and heads (toilets). In addition, *Alliance* could carry more fresh water, had greater cold storage for food, and an air-conditioning system. Fully fuelled, *Alliance* could travel up to 15,000 miles.

Above: HMS *Alliance* (as *P417*) underway on Sea Trials off Barrow-in-Furness, August 1946.

Above right: HMS *Alliance* coming alongside after a week 'snorting' in the Atlantic, 1947.

Below: HMS *Alliance* underway, 1947.

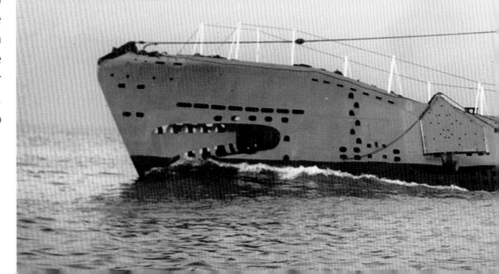

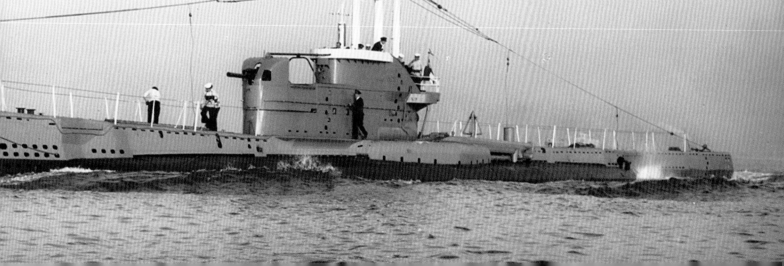

THE COLD WAR

In the latter stages of World War Two, it was apparent that with improvements in radar detection and the capability of anti-submarine aircraft, a submarine on the surface was becoming more vulnerable to detection and attack. Submarines needed to be able to remain submerged for much longer periods in order to minimise the chance of detection. *Alliance* was therefore constructed with a snort mast that enabled the submarine to remain submerged at periscope depth while running her diesels and charging her batteries. The necessity to surface under cover of darkness was therefore much reduced. Shortly after her commissioning in 1947, *Alliance* conducted a record-breaking passage of three weeks continuously submerged. It was headline news and, for a short period, *Alliance* held the World Record for the longest time a submarine had spent underwater.

O Class submarine underway at sea. View of officer on the bridge.

Left: HMS *Alliance* post modification underway. Camouflaged. 1967.

Below: HMS *Alliance* post modification entering Malta.1965.

THE CREW

ROLES

HMS *Alliance* had a crew of five officers and 60 men. The Captain had absolute authority over the submarine but at the same time lived in extremely close quarters to even the most junior members of the crew. The second in command, or First Lieutenant, was known by the crew as the 'Jimmy' and had responsibility for the day-to-day running of the submarine. *Alliance* was operated on a three-watch rota, which meant that while a third of the crew were at work, the rest were either sleeping or off duty – reading, writing letters home or playing cards. At Action stations and Diving stations, all the crew were at work.

Alliance is technically very complex and the crew needed a wide range of skills to operate the submarine. The largest contingent of the crew were Junior Ratings who performed the routine tasks of operating the submarine; they were typically in their early 20s. The Senior Ratings, the Petty and Chief Petty

Above: HMS *Alliance*. Interior. Crew members in the mess. Note the projector. Taken whilst en route to Singapore, 1964.

Right: HMS *Alliance*. Crew members relaxing in their mess after 1947 snort cruise. Tom Brunyee (on right) wrote 120 letters during the trip.

Officers – who supervised the Junior Ratings and were often highly skilled technicians – were often able to fix problems at sea and keep the submarine operational. Specific technical skills included mechanical and electrical engineering, wireless communications, navigation, SONAR operation and weapons engineering.

THE CREW

SLEEPING

Forward of the Control Room there were four messes for the men and the Wardroom for the officers. In the messes the crew ate their meals, slept and relaxed. The largest mess was home to 30 of the Junior Ratings. The second largest, the Stokers' Mess, was for those men who worked in the Engine Room. The smaller messes were for the Petty Officers and Engine Room Artificers (ERAs), reflecting their specialist skills and seniority.

The four main messes were not big enough to sleep all of the crew so a further 12 bunks were fitted in the main passageway. The torpedo compartments at the bow and stern also provided accommodation space. When *Alliance* was first commissioned, the torpedo crews slung hammocks from the deck head, but in later years bunks were fitted right next to the torpedo racks and the men slept alongside the weapons. The officers were accommodated in the Wardroom next to the Control

Above: HMS *Auriga*. Fore ends. Roy Cheshire on the right looking over his left shoulder. Singapore, 1966.
Below: The Wardroom, which acted as the Ship's Office as well the sleeping quarters for the officers.

TO OPERATE W.C. DISCHARGE.

1. CHARGE AIR BOTTLE AND OPEN SEA AND N.R. VALVES.
2. OPEN FLUSH INLET VALVE WITH CARE.
3. FREE LEVER AND BRING TO PAUSE.
4. BRING LEVER TO FLUSHING.
5. BRING LEVER TO DISCHARGE.
6. BRING LEVER TO PAUSE.
7. RETURN LEVER TO NORMAL AND LOCK.
8. CLOSE ALL VALVES.

Room. Although just as cramped as the other messes, it was more attractively furnished. The officers were not entitled to the daily rum issue but the Wardroom did have its own drinks cabinet.

WASHING AND HEADS

Alliance carried enough fresh water for drinking and limited washing; while the men could brush their teeth there was not enough for laundry or showers. The crew would seldom shave and rarely changed their clothes, perhaps only changing underwear and socks weekly. They slept in sleeping bags or hammocks while fully clothed – no sheets or pyjamas! Sewage was collected in a tank and discharged overboard by pressurising the tank until the pressure within exceeded the sea pressure outside. Once the sewage had been discharged, the tank had to be depressurised before the toilets (or 'heads') could be used again. This involved venting the pressure back into the submarine – a very smelly process!

THE CREW

COOKING AND EATING

The small galley in Alliance was run by the Cook and his assistant. Food was a very important part of life on board the submarine and a good chef was an important factor in maintaining crew morale. The Cook had to produce three meals each day for nearly 70 men, sometimes offering two choices. Typically, one Cook would work during the day preparing and serving meals, while the other worked during the night making bread.

Space on a submarine was always at a premium and although *Alliance* had a number of store rooms for provisions, much of the fresh food was stored wherever there was room for it. Sometimes tinned food was stored on the decks and even in the main passageway. The tins would be covered with layers of hardboard so the crew could walk over it, which was known as double decking. The submarine would sail with as much fresh bread and vegetables as possible, but this could perish very quickly in the hot, damp interior of the submarine so fresh food was eaten first, followed by tinned and frozen food for the later stages of a patrol.

Each mess provided a man to help with food preparation, which usually meant peeling potatoes. Meals were served from the galley and taken back to the messes to be eaten. Those carrying the food had to negotiate their way through the Control Room – a particularly difficult task at night when the Control Room would be darkened. The messes drew up a rota for washing up the dishes. Tea and coffee would be made using water from the boiler located at the head of the main passageway. The Wardroom officers had the same food as the men, but had a steward who organised the meals and did all their clearing up.

Above left: HMS *Alliance*. Tot Time. Chief Coxswain Thompson issuing rum.

Above: HMS *Alliance*. Cook in the Galley.

Above: Crew members washing up.

Left: HMS *Alliance*. Crew members in the fore ends at meal time. Far East, November 1964.

Below right: The ERAs' mess at tot time.

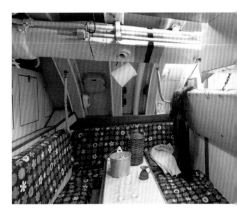

THE CAPTAIN'S CABIN

Immediately above the Control Room was the Captain's Cabin. The location of the Cabin in the Conning Tower was unique to the A Class and was not a feature of any other British submarines. When a submarine is on the surface, captains are frequently being called to the Bridge (at the top of the Conning Tower). With the Cabin located close to the Bridge it was thought it would make the Captain's job easier In practice, this did not prove practical and captains of A Class submarines spent most of their very limited spare time camped out in the Wardroom. This could be awkward – captains of Royal Navy ships are not members of the Wardroom so, in theory at least, could be refused entry! The Captain was on call 24 hours a day and got little sleep.

Right: HMS *Alliance* leaving Canada for the UK, 1958.
Insert: The Captain's Cabin.

THE BRIDGE

The top of the Conning Tower, or fin, is known as the Bridge. When *Alliance* was on the surface, her navigation was primarily controlled from the Bridge. The Bridge was also a vital observation point from where lookouts would be constantly watching the horizon and the sky for the presence of hostile ships and aircraft. The Bridge was equipped with compasses and an intercom so it could communicate with the Control Room, since the crew below continued to steer the submarine under the direction of the officer of the watch on the Bridge. Effective communication between Bridge and Control Room was so important that *Alliance* and many later submarines continued to be fitted with the voice pipe, which could be used if the intercom failed – as sometimes happened when the Bridge was washed over by waves or rain.

Main image: View from the bridge.
Right: HMS *Alliance* Lt. 'Darcy' Burdett (CO) on the bridge, 1950.

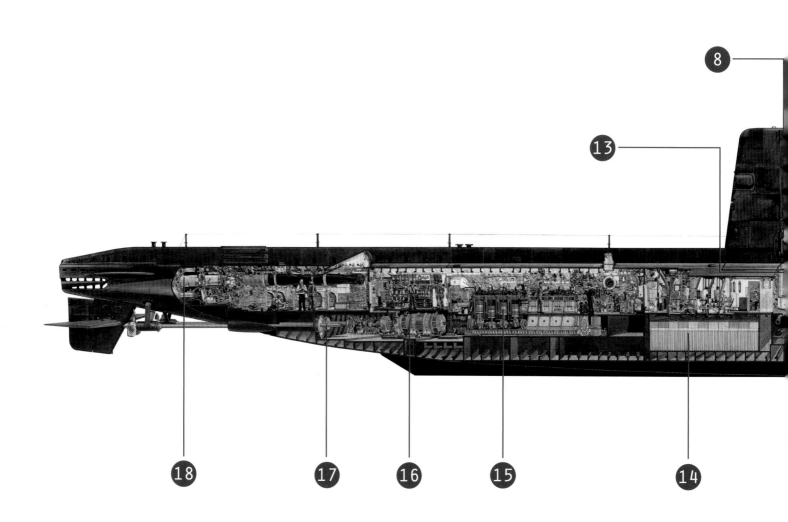

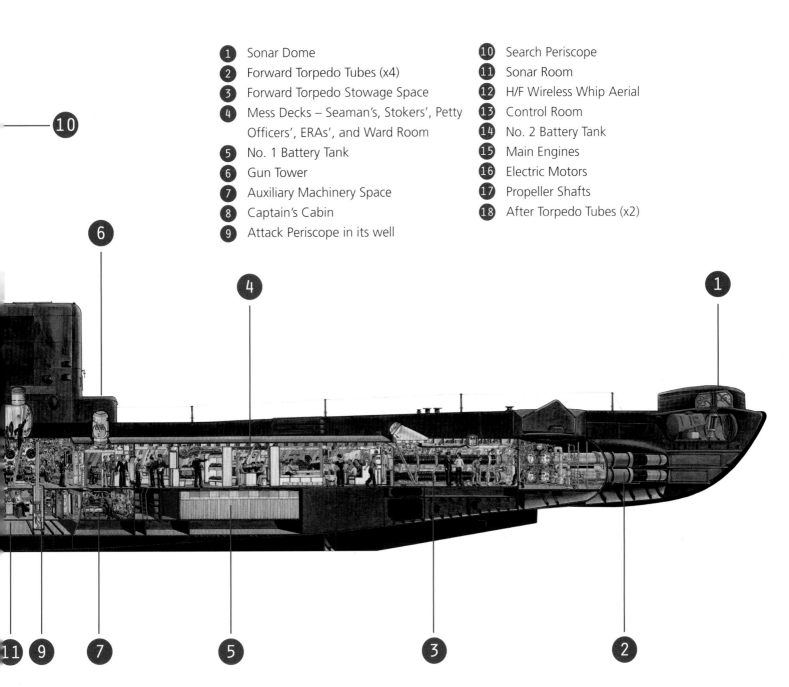

1. Sonar Dome
2. Forward Torpedo Tubes (x4)
3. Forward Torpedo Stowage Space
4. Mess Decks – Seaman's, Stokers', Petty Officers', ERAs', and Ward Room
5. No. 1 Battery Tank
6. Gun Tower
7. Auxiliary Machinery Space
8. Captain's Cabin
9. Attack Periscope in its well
10. Search Periscope
11. Sonar Room
12. H/F Wireless Whip Aerial
13. Control Room
14. No. 2 Battery Tank
15. Main Engines
16. Electric Motors
17. Propeller Shafts
18. After Torpedo Tubes (x2)

HOW ALLIANCE DIVES AND SURFACES

DIVING The Forward and After hydroplanes are set to dive positions.

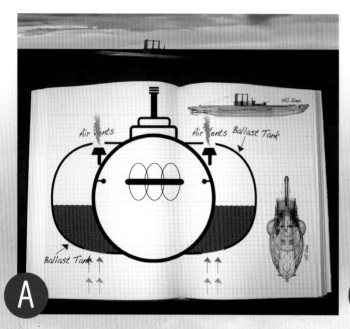

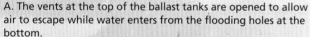

A

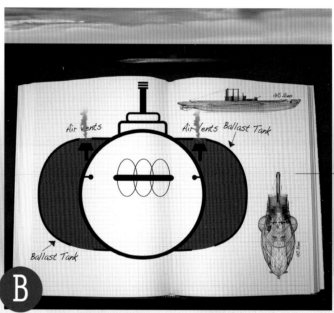

B

A. The vents at the top of the ballast tanks are opened to allow air to escape while water enters from the flooding holes at the bottom.

B. The water is now able to enter through the flooding holes at the bottom of the ballast tanks forcing out the air and the submarine dives below the surface.

SURFACING The Forward and After hydroplanes are set to surface positions.

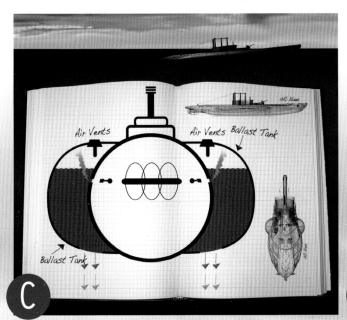

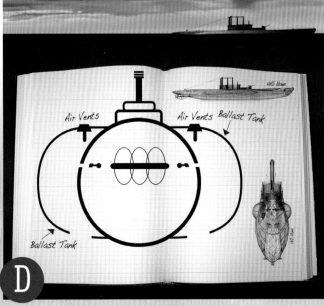

C. The vents at the top of the ballast tanks are closed and high pressure air from inside the pressure hull is used to force the water out of the flooding holes at the bottom.

D. The water is now forced out through the flooding holes at the bottom of the ballast tanks and the boat rises to the surface.

HMS *Alliance*. Diving. Bridge and periscopes in view. View from port beam.

THE CONTROL ROOM

The Control Room is referred to as the nerve centre of the submarine because so much of the equipment and crew charged with operating every aspect of the submarine was concentrated here. Observation, navigation, diving, surfacing, setting the course and speed of the submarine, and conducting attacks was directed from the Control Room. *Alliance*'s Attack Periscope, used specifically for torpedo attack, and the much more powerful Search Periscope dominate the Control Room layout. When not in use, they were lowered into the deep wells that go right down to the keel.

Alliance's helm, or steering position, is in the Control Room and was originally fitted with a traditional wooden steering wheel. Both the helm and hydroplane lever wheels were replaced in the 1950s. By contrast, the blowing panel that controls the ballast and trim tanks so vital to *Alliance*'s buoyancy and ability to dive are largely unchanged since the submarine was built in 1945. The Control Room, like many parts

of the submarine, contains a mix of different equipment designs that reflect the submarine's World War Two origins and the later modernisation undertaken in the Cold War period.

Right: Young visitors to HMS *Alliance* at the helm and the hydroplane controls.

Below: The Control Room of HMS *Alliance*, showing the search periscope.

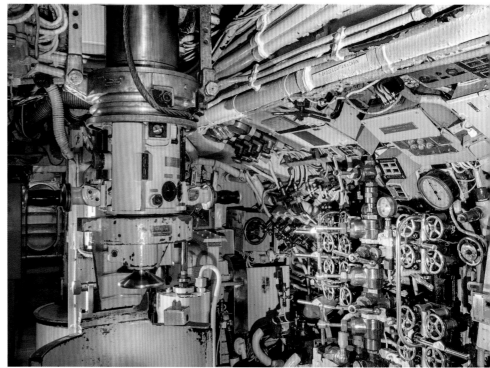

SONAR, COMMUNICATION AND NAVIGATION

Alliance was originally fitted with a sound-detection system. This hydrophone was fitted at the front of the keel and helped identify the presence of surface ships and submarines from the noise they made. During the modernisation of 1958, *Alliance* had a SONAR (Sound Navigation & Ranging) system fitted in the bow under a large dome. This was a more sensitive device that could listen and also produce active sound pulses for detection. The SONAR Room was situated immediately below the Control Room.

The Radar and Radio Offices are situated at the after end of the Control Room. The telescopic radar mast could be used at periscope depth and was raised only when absolutely necessary. *Alliance* could receive radio messages while submerged on a special submarine VLF (Very Low Frequency) broadcast; no aerial had to be exposed above the surface. An aerial was raised to transmit signals on HF (High Frequency) but the risk of being detected by the enemy meant that while on patrol only urgent signals, such as enemy sighting reports,

were ever transmitted. Warning of enemy ships and aircraft using search radar was given by a special ESM (Electronic Support Measure) mast, particularly useful at night when an enemy aircraft might not be sighted through the periscope.

Navigating *Alliance* presented a particular challenge especially when long periods were spent beneath the water. On the surface or at periscope depth, a position could be established by conventional means such as visual fixing, astronomic observation or radio-navigation aids. When dived, the submarine's position is estimated by 'dead reckoning' – this means plotting course, speed and depth; corrected for any known tides or currents – this provides a best guess 'estimated position'. In wartime, submarines are allocated patrol areas to avoid being attacked by friendly ships and submarines – another reason why accurate navigation was vital.

Above right: HMS *Alliance*. Wireless Office. Rating taking a message.
Right: The Wireless Office.

THE ENGINE ROOM

Alliance is powered by two supercharged diesel engines, each generating 2,000 horsepower. The engines weigh 30 tons each and are connected by the clutch mechanism to the electric motors, and then finally to the propeller shafts. *Alliance* was one of the first British submarines to be built with a mast consisting of a long steel tube like a snorkel, which was raised to the surface and allowed the engines to draw in air and also to expel the exhaust fumes while running submerged. This process was called 'snorting'. This system enabled the submarine to run its engines and charge its battery whilst dived at periscope depth. When *Alliance* was on the surface or snorting with the engines running, the noise was such that the Engine Room crew could not hear each other and had to communicate using hand signals.

Below left: The engine clutch.
Below: Pressure gauges above the engine.

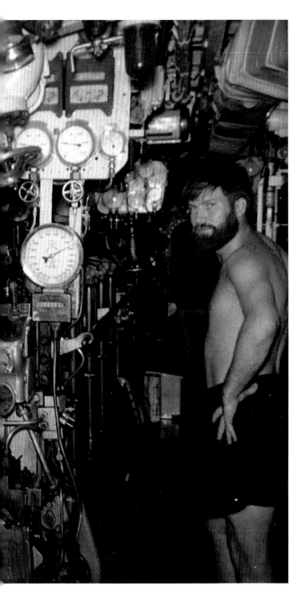

Above: HMS *Alliance*. Crew members in the Engine Room. Far East, November 1964.

Right: View from the Motor Room into the Engine Room.

THE MOTOR ROOM AND BATTERIES

When *Alliance* was dived she was propelled by electric motors turning each propeller shaft. The motors were powered by batteries consisting of 226 lead acid cells, each weighing half a ton, stored in two tanks below the deck level forward and aft of the Control Room. The motors were controlled from switch gear located just aft of the engines. Unlike the main engines, the motors could also be run in reverse, which meant that they were very useful for manoeuvring the submarine when coming alongside in harbour.

Preserving and managing the power in the batteries was a major concern for the Captain. If the motors were run at full power, *Alliance* could reach an underwater speed of more than 10 knots but had a range of just 16 miles; if the speed was reduced to 3 knots then the range went up to 90 miles. The Captain had to judge whether it was safe to charge the batteries – which required the submarine to be on the surface – or to raise its snort mast above the surface. When clutched into the main engines, the motors also acted as generators for recharging the batteries. If the battery was allowed to be discharged to a low level, the submarine's operational capability was much reduced. When lead acid batteries are being charged, hydrogen gas is generated, which is dangerous if not managed carefully. *Alliance* had a sophisticated hydrogen-ventilation system to expel the gas while charging. However, the inherent dangers of the technology were tragically illustrated in March 1968 when, while charging batteries in harbour, there was an explosion on board *Alliance* that tore through the forward mess areas killing crewman Raymond Kimber and seriously injuring several others.

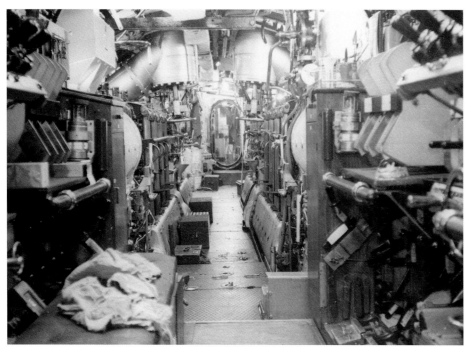

Right: HMS *Astute*. Motor Room, February 1956.
Left: HMS *Alaric*. Motor Room, 1952.

WEAPONS

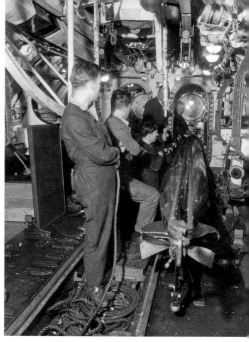

HMS *Aurochs*. Fore ends. Torpedo being loaded.

Alliance was constructed with six torpedo tubes at the bow and two at the stern. Two of the six tubes in the bow were external to the pressure hull, which meant that while on patrol the crew had no access to them. The external tubes were loaded with torpedoes in harbour and could be fired, but not re-loaded. The forward torpedo stowage compartment could accommodate a total of six reload torpedoes, meaning that on a war patrol *Alliance* sailed with 12 torpedoes in the forward torpedo compartment. The two tubes in the stern provided a further two weapons plus four reloads on the racks.

When first commissioned in 1947, *Alliance* was armed with the Mark VIII torpedo. The Mark VIII had entered service in 1921 and was remarkable for its longevity, finally being withdrawn from service in 1984. There were various versions of the Mark VIII but it remained a fairly reliable diesel engine-propelled weapon with a charge of 365 kilos of high explosive, capable of 45 knots and a range of up to 5,000 yards.

However, the Mark VIII had been designed primarily for use against surface ships at relatively close range and not for the more elusive target of another submerged submarine. In order to equip *Alliance* for her Cold War role in countering the Soviet submarine threat, she was fitted with equipment that enabled her to fire the new Mark 23 wire-guided electrically powered torpedoes.

During World War Two, the deck gun was almost as important as the torpedoes. When originally built, *Alliance* was equipped with a deck gun for attacking targets that didn't justify the use of an expensive torpedo. The key factor in submarine gun actions was surprise and speed. Gun crews were trained to fire the first round within seconds of the submarine breaking surface. Once on the surface, a submarine was relatively vulnerable and, therefore, for a gun action to be successful, the submarine needed to overcome a target with rapid well-aimed fire as quickly as possible.

In addition to a 4 inch deck gun, *Alliance* was originally fitted with twin Oerlikon cannons at the rear of the Conning Tower, which were used for countering attacks by aircraft. The 1958 modernisation saw the removal of all the guns along with the open Conning Tower. This was intended to improve the submarine's underwater performance. In the Cold War period, British submarines did not need a gun to attack small merchant vessels, but needed to be able to use stealth to shadow underwater targets and, thanks to the snort technology, avoid being detected on the surface.

Above: HMS *Alliance* alongside. 1950. High view looking down on to bridge and gun.

Above left: The forward torpedo compartment. As well as storing torpedoes and food supplies, crew members would sling their hammocks.

Left: Modified A Class. 4in deck gun.

Below: HMS *Aurochs*. Torpedo being loaded through the fore hatch.

ESCAPE

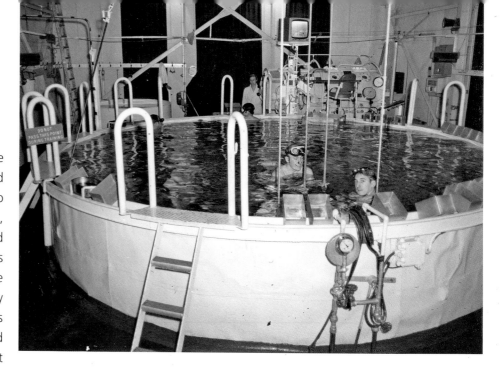

The Royal Navy's first submarines, the Holland Class, built in the early 1900s, had the distinction of having suffered no major accidents. In subsequent years, a number of tragedies highlighted the need for better escape techniques and equipment. In 1927 the primitive Hall-Rees equipment was replaced by the Davis Submerged Escape Apparatus (DSEA). The DSEA provided pressurised oxygen during escape. This equipment also acted as a buoyancy aid for survivors on reaching the surface. The danger of breathing oxygen under pressure was not fully understood. Survival suits were eventually introduced to help avoid the effects of hypothermia.

By the time *Alliance* entered service the decision had been taken that men must be taught to escape without using any breathing apparatus. Both torpedo stowage compartments in the stern and forward parts of *Alliance* were fitted with an escape hatch and an emergency breathing system. A canvas trunk could be lowered beneath each escape hatch to help facilitate escape. The compartment would be flooded with seawater to equal the water pressure outside the submarine and once this was achieved the escape hatch could be opened allowing the men to make their escape. The crew of *Alliance* had to carry out routine escape training in the shore facility at HMS *Dolphin*. In 1970 escapes in modern suits were safely made from a British submarine from the record depth of 600 feet.

Above: Interior view at the top of the tank.
Right: The Submarine Escape Training Tank at HMS *Dolphin*.
Far right: The Twill Trunk.

Right: Escape trial on board HMS *Sleuth*.

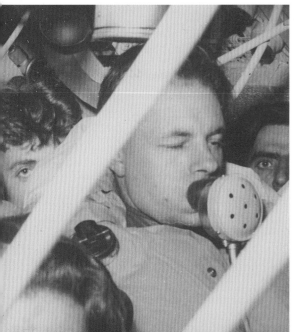

MEMORIAL

Since 1904 over 5,300 Royal Navy submariners have lost their lives while serving in British submarines – with a casualty rate of about 35 per cent during World War Two. So often when a submarine was lost, there were no survivors. To add to the sorrow of the grieving families, the cause of the loss frequently remained unknown and the exact location of the sunken submarine remained a mystery. In 1979, HMS *Alliance* was the only surviving submarine from the World War Two era and the Royal Navy Submarine Service decided that she should be preserved not only as an historic submarine, but also as a memorial.

HMS *Alliance*. Floral tributes to HMS *Affray* victims.

THE ORIGINS OF THE ROYAL NAVY SUBMARINE SERVICE

Between 1860 and the 1900 the Royal Navy received in the order of 260 different proposals for the construction of submarine craft. However, the Admiralty, while taking every opportunity to observe and assess the progress that other countries made with submarine designs during the latter half the 19th century, refrained from taking any practical steps of their own. Finally, after significant achievements by the French Navy in submarine development, the Royal Navy took decisive action.

By far the most sophisticated and well-engineered submarine designs available in 1900 were those of the Irish-American inventor John Philip Holland, now regarded as the 'father of the submarine'. The Admiralty bought John Holland's designs via the American Electric Boat Company that employed Holland, and five submarines of the Holland Class were constructed at the Barrow-in-Furness shipbuilding yard in Cumbria. HM Submarine Torpedo Boat *No. 1*, which became known as *Holland 1*, was launched in October 1901 and, along with the other four submarines of the class, became one of the lead ships of a whole new branch of the Royal Navy.

Holland 1 is now preserved at the Royal Navy Submarine Museum. The pioneering trail blazed by the Holland Class led to the rapid development of submarine design in the Royal Navy. At 120 tons, the Holland Class were capable of no more than harbour defence – but 13 years later at the outbreak of World War One, the Royal Navy had a fleet of submarines capable of operating in the Baltic and the Mediterranean.

In the Museum's historical galleries you can trace the great achievements of the Royal Navy Submarine Service through the two world wars and experience the personal human stories of Royal Navy submariners.

Above: *Holland 1* on display at The Royal Navy Submarine Museum.

Below: HM Submarine Torpedo Boat *No. 1* (aka *Holland 1*) underway with seven crew on deck.

SUBMARINE PIONEERS, WORLD WARS ONE AND TWO

Above: HM Submarine Torpedo Boat *No. 1* (aka *Holland 1*) underway.
Close-up of crew with Petty Officer William Waller, coxswain at the wheel.

Right: HMS *X24* X craft on display at The Royal Navy Submarine Museum.

Below: HMS *Saracen* returning to Algiers with her Jolly Roger flying. 1943.

Above: HMS *X24* in Balta Firth, Shetlands, on return from the attack on Bergen, September 1944.

Below: HMS *E11* returning from the Dardanelles. 1915.

Above Left: Lieutenant Commander Martin Eric Nasmith VC. (HMS *E11* – World War One.)

Above Right: Lieutenant Commander Malcolm David Wanklyn VC. (HMS *Upholder* – World War Two.)

THE COLD WAR PERIOD

Submarine warfare changed dramatically in the Cold War period. In 1960, Britain launched HMS *Dreadnought*, its first nuclear-powered submarine. A few years later, in 1966, the Royal Navy Submarine Service took on the enormous technical challenge of maintaining Britain's strategic nuclear deterrent in the form of the Resolution Class submarines equipped with the Polaris Ballistic Missile System, and also had to direct its submarine fleet toward countering the potential threat from the vast navy and submarine fleet of the Soviet Union.

Right: Polaris missile launch conducted from Resolution Class submarine.

Below: HMS *Dreadnought* underway at sea.